FOUR WARS *of* 1812

D. PETER MACLEOD

with the Canadian War Museum 1812 *team:*
ERIC FERNBERG, GARETH NEWFIELD, GLENN OGDEN, AND MYRIAM PROULX

FOUR WARS *of*
1812

Douglas & McIntyre
D&M PUBLISHERS INC.
Vancouver/Toronto/Berkeley

CANADIAN WAR MUSEUM

Douglas & McIntyre
An imprint of D&M Publishers Inc.
2323 Quebec Street, Suite 201
Vancouver BC Canada V5T 4S7
www.douglas-mcintyre.com

Canadian Museum of Civilization Corporation
100, rue Laurier Street
Gatineau QC Canada K1A 0M8

Cataloguing data available from Library and Archives Canada
ISBN 978-1-77100-050-5 (pbk.)

Editing by Shirarose Wilensky
Cover and interior design by Peter Cocking
Front cover image: John David Kelly, *The Battle of Queenston Heights,
13 October 1812*, 1896, Library and Archives Canada, C-000273K,
Acc. No. 1954-153-1. Back cover image: Carlton Chapman,
Engagement between the U.S. Frigate Constitution *and HMS
Guerriere*, 1895, Collection of the New York Historical Society
Maps by Eric Leinberger
Printed and bound in Canada by Friesens
Distributed in the U.S. by Publishers Group West
Also published in French as *Les quatre guerres de 1812*,
translated by Christian Bérubé and edited by Myriam Afriat.

We gratefully acknowledge the financial support of the Canada
Council for the Arts, the British Columbia Arts Council,
the Province of British Columbia through the Book Publishing
Tax Credit, and the Government of Canada through the Canada
Book Fund for our publishing activities.

Douglas & McIntyre is committed to reducing the consumption
of old-growth forests in the books it publishes. This book is
one step towards that goal.

The Canadian War Museum would like to thank the following sponsors of *1812*,
the national travelling exhibition marking the bicentennial of the War of 1812.

NATIONAL PRESENTING SPONSOR

NATIONAL SUPPORTING SPONSOR

ancestry.ca

CONTENTS

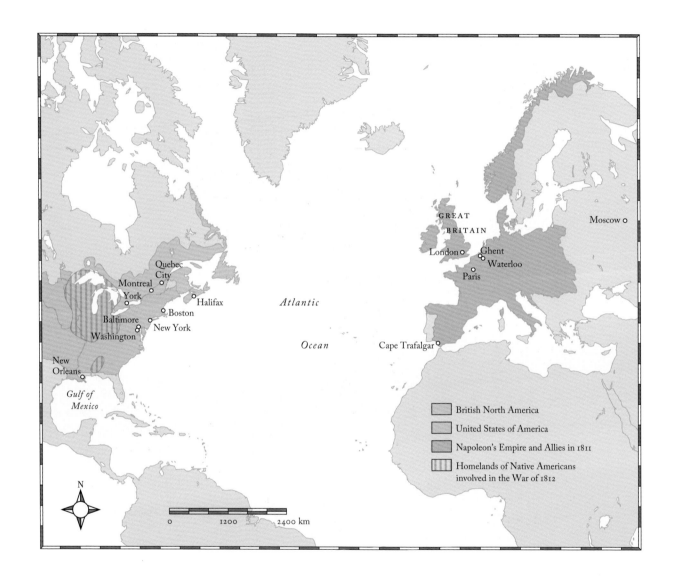

GREAT
BRITAIN

Moscow o

London o o Ghent
           Waterloo
      o Paris

Quebec
City
Montreal o
York o
         o Halifax
Baltimore o Boston
Washington o New York

New
Orleans o

Gulf of
Mexico

Atlantic

Ocean

Cape Trafalgar o

N

0   1200   2400 km

British North America

United States of America

Napoleon's Empire and Allies in 1811

Homelands of Native Americans
involved in the War of 1812

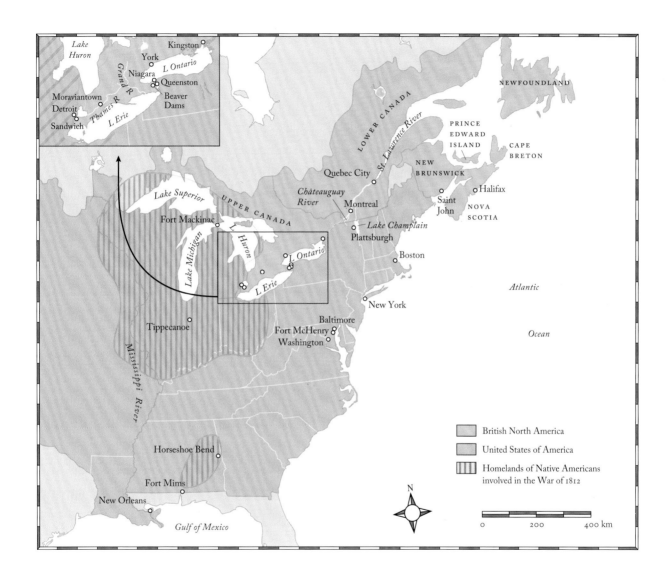

Lake Huron

Kingston

York

Niagara

L Ontario

Moraviantown

Queenston

Detroit

Beaver Dams

Sandwich

Grand R

Thames R

L Erie

Lake Superior

UPPER CANADA

Fort Mackinac

Lake Michigan

L Huron

Mississippi River

L Ontario

L Erie

LOWER CANADA

St. Lawrence River

NEWFOUNDLAND

PRINCE EDWARD ISLAND

CAPE BRETON

NEW BRUNSWICK

Quebec City

Châteauguay River

Montreal

Lake Champlain

Saint John

NOVA SCOTIA

Halifax

Plattsburgh

Boston

New York

Atlantic

Ocean

Tippecanoe

Baltimore

Fort McHenry

Washington

Horseshoe Bend

Fort Mims

New Orleans

Gulf of Mexico

N

British North America

United States of America

Homelands of Native Americans involved in the War of 1812

0   200   400 km

INTRODUCTION

THE WAR OF 1812 is best known as the conflict between Great Britain and the United States that lasted from 1812 until 1815.

For more than a decade before it began, this conflict had been a war waiting to happen. Britain, which had been at war with France for almost a generation, placed a higher priority on winning the war in Europe than on avoiding war with the United States. There was widespread outrage in the United States over Britain's interference with American merchant ships and warships at sea, in its attempts to obtain sailors for the Royal Navy and to control American trade with France. Moreover, many Americans suspected that Britain was supporting Native Americans who resisted American westward expansion. (The term "Native Americans" here refers to First Peoples living along the American settlement frontier, mostly inside the borders of the nineteenth-century United States.)

In June 1812, the American government declared war on Great Britain. Canadians, including Canadian First Peoples, became involved when Americans invaded Canada, the only part of the British Empire they could easily attack. Many Native Americans joined the war on Britain's side to obtain British support for the defence of their homelands against the United States.

For two and a half years, fighting raged in the Great Lakes region, Lake Champlain, the American Atlantic and Gulf coasts, and on the high seas. When it became apparent to both the British and the Americans that neither side could overcome the other, they negotiated the Treaty of Ghent. This treaty ended the war in 1815 but left Native American territory exposed to continued American encroachment.

That is one way of looking at the War of 1812 but not the only way. All participants in all wars, and their descendants, have their own perspectives on events.

These perspectives are not about right or wrong. They are about what a group of people think is important in a war—or any other historical episode—and what meaning it holds for them. If a group considers an episode to be important enough, then its members incorporate it into a collective narrative, a fact-based mythology that helps to define them as a people or a nation. To create these narratives, they emphasize events and circumstances that they believe reflect their sense of who they are and use them to create their own version of history.

Canadians and Americans have used the War of 1812 as a source of nation-building narratives, centred on their distinct stories of the war. But all four major participants—Americans, Britons, Canadians, and Native Americans—fought and remembered their own War of 1812.

For Canadians, the War of 1812 was about American invasions. For Americans, it was about standing up to Britain. For the British, it was an annoying sideshow to the Napoleonic Wars. For Native Americans, it was a desperate struggle for freedom and independence as they fought to defend their homelands.

1

THE AMERICAN WAR

And the star-spangled banner in triumph doth wave,

O'er the land of the free and the home of the brave.

FRANCIS SCOTT KEY, 1814

A VIEW of the PRESIDENTS HOUSE in the CITY of WASHINGTON

after the Conflagration of the 24.th August 1814.

A VIEW OF THE PRESIDENTS HOUSE
British troops burned the White House in 1814 to retaliate for
the burning of the Upper Canadian Legislative Assembly building
in York (Toronto) by American invaders the year before.

A SYMBOL OF VICTORY

THIS SOUVENIR T-shirt from Fort McHenry, where the repulse of the British attack inspired the writing of America's national anthem, provides a fine example of a symbol of American perceptions of victory.

For Americans, the War of 1812 was a triumphant second War of Independence. Seeing themselves as bullied and oppressed by the British Empire, they fought back, forcing the world to respect American sovereignty and American power. Marauding British troops captured Washington, but bold American sailors taught the Royal Navy a lesson at sea and on Lake Erie, and the war ended with a great American victory at the Battle of New Orleans.

FREEDOM OF THE SEAS

THIS ENGRAVING, showing a Royal Navy boarding party forcibly removing sailors from an American ship, portrays a major American grievance against Britain.

In the years prior to the outbreak of war, the British had infringed upon American sovereignty by stopping and boarding American vessels at sea to search for sailors who could be impressed into (compelled to join) the Royal Navy. British naval boarding parties frequently encountered former Britons who had immigrated to the United States. They refused to recognize the naturalized citizenship of these Americans and treated them as if they were still British subjects. In 1807, the two countries nearly went to war when HMS *Leopard* fired on the USS *Chesapeake*, forced the American frigate to surrender, and carried off four members of the crew.

At the same time, Britain undermined the American economy and American sovereignty by seizing any American ship that sailed to ports in the Napoleonic Empire without first stopping in Britain to pay duty on its cargo.

THE AMERICAN FRONTIER

THIS CARICATURE faithfully reflects the widely held American opinion that the British were using Native Americans to wage a vicious proxy war against settlers on the western frontier.

For Americans who held this opinion, Native Americans taking up arms to defend their homelands did so at the instigation of British officers and Indian agents, who provided the arms and munitions that made war against the United States possible. This was not the case, but, in the hands of American "War Hawks," it became a strong argument in favour of war with Britain.

On June 1, 1812, U.S. president James Madison sent a message to Congress asking for a declaration of war. He cited Britain's impressment of American sailors, attempts to control American international trade, and support for Native Americans. Congress assented, with the House of Representatives voting seventy-nine to forty-nine and the Senate nineteen to thirteen for war. On June 18, the United States formally declared war on Great Britain.

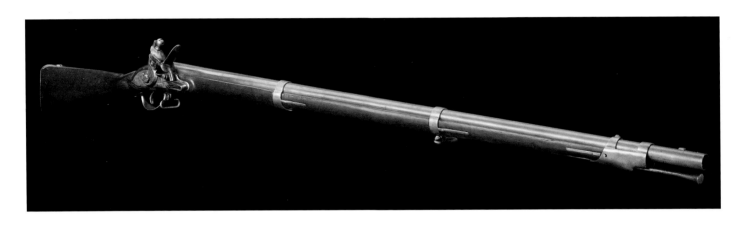

LAND BATTLES

When American regular soldiers marched into battle, most carried the U.S. Model 1795 flintlock musket, the standard American infantry weapon.

Prevented by the Royal Navy from striking Britain directly, the Americans chose to fight Britain on land by invading Canada. They went to war in 1812 expecting a quick, decisive victory. In 1775, during the War of Independence, American rebels had made a rapid advance to Quebec and besieged the city. Although that effort had failed, thirty-seven years later many American leaders believed that history was about to repeat itself. Thomas Jefferson, in particular, famously proclaimed in August 1812 that "the acquisition of Canada this year, as far as the neighbourhood of Quebec, will be a mere matter of marching, and will give us experience for the attack on Halifax the next and the final expulsion of England from the American continent."

Instead, American armies in Canada and ships on the Great Lakes won many battles but few campaigns. The American army became more professional fighting in Canada, but it never came close to threatening British possession of the colony.

AMERICAN VICTORIES AT SEA

O<small>N THE</small> Atlantic Ocean and Lake Erie, American efforts met with greater success and helped to create a powerful mythology. This painting of the dismasted H<small>MS</small> *Guerriere* adrift off the port bow of the U<small>SS</small> *Constitution*, following a ship-to-ship action in the Atlantic, provides a fine illustration of how Americans remember the war at sea.

The U.S. Navy was minute, compared with the Royal Navy, but highly skilled. Ship for ship, American vessels were frequently more effective than their British counterparts. When frigates of the two navies met in action, the result was generally an American victory. There were too few American frigates and too few American victories to threaten British control of the sea or break the British blockade of the eastern seaboard, but ships like the *Constitution* laid the foundations of a proud naval tradition that has continued to the present.

On the Great Lakes, the capture by Commodore Oliver Hazard Perry of an entire British squadron at the Battle of Lake Erie in 1813 gave the U.S. Navy control of that crucial transportation link. The British, no longer able to supply their forces in southwest Upper Canada, evacuated the region. Pursuing Americans shattered a Native American coalition, led by Tecumseh and allied to the British, at the Battle of the Thames. The U.S. Navy thereby made a notable contribution to the conquest of the American west, but it could neither prevent the British from recovering their lost territory nor secure Lake Ontario or the upper lakes. The U.S. Navy still remembers the Battle of Lake Erie and Perry's famous dispatch announcing the victory: "We have met the enemy and they are ours."

continued overleaf >

American sailor David Bunnell, serving aboard the brig *Lawrence*, preserved harsher recollections of the battle in his memoirs.

The deck was in a shocking predicament. Death had been very busy. It was one continued gore of blood and carnage—the dead and dying were strewed in every direction over it—for it was impossible to take the wounded below as fast as they fell… During the action a shot struck a man in the head who was standing close by me; his brains flew so thick in my face that I was for some time blinded and for a few minutes was at a loss to ascertain whether it was him or me that was killed.

facing:

JOHN BULL AND THE BALTIMOREANS.
This American cartoon trumpets the defeat of
the British attack on Baltimore in 1814.

A VIEW of the BOMBARDMENT of Fort McHenry, near Baltimore, by the British fleet, taken from the Observatory, under the Command of Admirals Cochrane, & Cockburn, on the morning of the 13th of Sep.r 1814 which lasted 24 hours, & thrown from 1500 to 1800 shells, in the Night attempted to land by forcing a passage up the ferry branch but were repulsed with great loss.

References.
A. Fort McHenry.
B. Lazaretto.
C. Saltrance House.
D. Admiral Ship's North Point.
E. Ferry and Fort.

WASHINGTON AND FORT McHENRY

THIS PRINT captures some of the drama of the British attack on Baltimore. For some American witnesses, the scene was terrifying but inspirational. Lieutenant John Harris of the U.S. Marine Corps wrote: "I think the handsomest sight I ever saw was during the bombarding to see the bombs and rockets flying and the firing from our three forts. It was much handsomer at night than in the day."

Others were more pessimistic. Phoebe Morris of Philadelphia wrote to her father that "they are making the bravest resistance but a letter has been received by Mr. Dallas which says that Baltimore must fall!... Tomorrow I shall be obliged to write the sad account of the defeat of Baltimore."

Aboard a ship anchored fifteen kilometres away, Baltimore lawyer Francis Scott Key spent the night watching the bombardment and wondering if the Americans had been defeated. But in the morning, he looked up the river and saw the Stars and Stripes still flying, proud and defiant. Key's relief was immediate and profound. As he later exclaimed to his brother-in-law, "Our flag was still there!"

Deeply moved, Keys wrote a poem, "Defence of Fort McHenry." Quickly set to music and first performed in public at Captain McCauley's tavern in Baltimore in October 1814, it became a popular patriotic song, "The Star-Spangled Banner." In 1931, "The Star-Spangled Banner" became the American national anthem. The poem and song, in turn, changed the status of the American flag from a simple national banner into a near-sacred symbol of America.

THE BATTLE OF NEW ORLEANS

THIS PAINTING by an artist serving in the American army depicts a British attack on a line of American fortifications during the Battle of New Orleans, an American triumph that brought the War of 1812 to what Americans consider to be a victorious conclusion.

Not particularly successful invading Canada, the Americans had done better defending their own territory. Although they failed to prevent the British from occupying Maine in 1814, American forces defeated a British invasion on Lake Champlain at the Battle of Plattsburgh, New York, in September of that year and won the last major battle of the war on January 8, 1815, at New Orleans.

AMERICA VICTORIOUS

THE ORIGINAL Star-Spangled Banner that flew over Fort McHenry during the British attack is now the most important artifact of the American War of 1812. On permanent display in the Smithsonian Institution's National Museum of American History, it serves as a symbol of American patriotism, American valour, and American victory.

Even before the end of hostilities, the war had come to be seen as a nation-building experience, a second American Revolution that gave America a national anthem and naval tradition and sanctified the American flag.

For future generations, the Battle of New Orleans and the Washington campaign, the latter culminating not in the burning of the White House but in the defence of Fort McHenry, became elements of a story of the emerging greatness of a new country. By extension, the War of 1812 came to be seen this way as well. The Americans may not have defeated Britain, but they had demonstrated that the British Empire could not defeat them either.

As the manager of an American historic site explained in 2007, "Certainly we won [the War of 1812]. Because if we hadn't, we'd be using loonies and toonies instead of dollar bills, wouldn't we?"

facing:
THE STAR-SPANGLED BANNER
This giant American flag is the original Star-Spangled Banner that flew
over Fort McHenry during the British bombardment in 1814.

2

THE BRITISH WAR

The King's government ... [has] most unequivocally expressed

to me their desire to preserve peace with the United States,

that they might, uninterrupted, pursue with the whole disposable

force of the country, the great[er] interest in Europe.

SIR GEORGE PREVOST,

Governor-in-chief of British North America, 1812

BRITAIN'S WAR WITH FRANCE

WHEN THE British think of the wars of the early nineteenth century, they remember battles like Trafalgar and Waterloo in their war against Napoleon Bonaparte, rather than the War of 1812. Napoleon's empire controlled much of the territory and resources of mainland Europe and posed a far greater threat to Britain than did the United States. When the War of 1812 broke out, Britain's goal in North America was not so much defeating the United States as defending Canada without compromising the war with France.

France had been Europe's paramount power for centuries. Its conversion into a revolutionary state and the expansion of Napoleon's empire had shattered the European balance of power and provoked a generation of war. As battles involving tens or hundreds of thousands of combatants raged across Europe, state after state had fallen before the French. Every alliance that sought to oppose Napoleon collapsed in failure and defeat. In the years prior to the outbreak of the War of 1812, Britain had faced an enormous French army posted just across the English Channel, poised to invade, and a continental blockade intended to break the British economy. Compared with this titanic conflict, fighting the United States was nothing more than an annoying sideshow.

The British did make a serious and successful effort to defend Canada and blockade the United States, but they never lost sight of their primary goal of defeating Napoleonic France.

BRITONS UNITED: THE WORLD CANNOT CONQUER.

Though Russia yields the well contested day, | Oh! let the Spirit of the Isle appear,
And Prussia sinks beneath the Tyrant's sway, | Nerve every arm and sharpen every spear!
England shall stand, amidst each ruin'd State | Let evil feuds — disgraceful discord — end,
If true herself — Impregnable and Great! | And ev'ry Briton, prove Britannia's friend!!

"What! shall they seek the Lion in his Den,
"And fright him there, and make him tremble there?
"O! let it not be said!

Publish'd Sept.r 1.1807. by LAURIE & WHITTLE, 53. Fleet Street, London.

BRITONS UNITED: THE WORLD CANNOT CONQUER.
Published in 1807, this cartoon showing a British soldier and sailor shaking hands
calls for unity in the face of the threat posed by Napoleon's French empire.

BLOCKADE AND IMPRESSMENT

ONE OF Britain's strongest weapons in the war with France was the merchant marine. Merchant vessels carried the commercial cargos that generated much of the wealth to finance the war against Napoleon, along with troops and supplies for military operations.

Lacking an army large enough to defeat the French, Britain relied upon naval power, financial support for European allies, and economic blockade to wage war on their adversary. Desperately short of sailors, Britain ignored American sovereignty and citizenship and resorted to impressing individuals it claimed as British subjects off American merchant ships and warships. At the same time, Britain attempted to control American shipping to enforce a blockade of Napoleon's European empire.

facing:
SIR GEORGE PREVOST
Sir George Prevost served as commander-in-chief of the British forces
in North America during the War of 1812. Without supplies and
reinforcements carried by the British merchant marine and escorted by the
Royal Navy, Prevost could not have defended Canada during the war.

NATIVE AMERICAN ALLIANCES

GREAT BRITAIN was alarmed by the possibility that the United States might invade Canada in response to these measures, so it maintained diplomatic contact with Native Americans, including those portrayed in this painting, *Deputation of Indians from the Mississippi Tribes*. In the event of war, Native Americans could be invaluable allies for Britain.

The British prudently refrained from encouraging these potential allies to make war on the United States. Given, however, that many Native Americans had been fighting the United States as recently as 1811, diplomatic relations with nations that might support the British in the event of an American war also increased the possibility that the United States would go to war with Britain.

The United States reacted to what Americans perceived as a long series of British provocations by declaring war on June 18, 1812. Anne Prevost, daughter of Sir George Prevost, governor-in-chief of British North America, recorded her reaction to the outbreak of war in her journal.

> June 25th: I was summoned in the midst of my French lesson to hear some news that had arrived. It was indeed an important piece of intelligence: "America has declared War against England." The news had arrived by an Express to some of the Quebec merchants.
>
> God forgive me! but I know well I felt anything but sorrow on hearing of an event which led to so much bloodshed and misery, and which was the source of all the calamities that have overwhelmed my family, and left me "alone on earth" to mourn over the past.

QUEBEC CITY AND HALIFAX

P AINTED IN 1840, *View from near the Officer Barrack* portrays the features that made Quebec City the linchpin of the British presence in Canada— powerful fortifications and a secure harbour.

The United States never came close to winning the War of 1812 because it never came close to taking Quebec City and Halifax, the keys to British control of Canada. Quebec City, Canada's Atlantic port, served as the point of entry for reinforcements and supplies from Britain to Lower and Upper Canada. In addition, Halifax provided an essential base of operations for the Royal Navy in North American waters.

Such was their importance that five years before the war, the British Secretary of State for War and the Colonies declared that should the United States ever capture one of these posts, Britain would send an expeditionary force to get it back.

> There are only two capital objects which could fully repay the expenditure and danger of an expedition. One, is the seizure of the town and harbour of Halifax in Nova Scotia, which could deprive His Majesty's fleet of the most important naval station in the North American continent; the other the capture of the fortress of Quebec, which would place them in the sovereignty of His Majesty's Canadian possessions.

FIGHTING THE WAR OF 1812

THIS COAT belonged to a Quebec resident serving in the 3rd Battalion, Quebec Militia, which was part of a combined force of British and Canadian regulars and Lower Canadian militia that garrisoned Quebec. The Quebec garrison never saw action but played an indispensable role by standing ready to defend their city should the Americans attack.

The British army fought the North American war in the interior by maintaining a strong garrison in Quebec and deploying a small army along the American frontiers with Upper and Lower Canada. The Royal Navy positioned small squadrons on the Great Lakes and Lake Champlain.

BLOCKADING AND RAIDING

THE PAINTING *HMS* Shannon *Leading Her Prize the American Frigate* Chesapeake *into Halifax* speaks to Halifax's role as a base for British naval operations against the American east coast.

While the British army defended Canada, the Royal Navy blockaded the United States. From Maine to Georgia, British warships kept watch off every American port. The blockade crippled American coastal and overseas trade and, with them, the American economy and government revenues.

In 1813, the British began raiding the American coast, targeting ports where Americans attempted to interfere with the blockade. They attacked ships and military and industrial centres. Residents who stood aside were left alone. Those who resisted risked having their property looted and burned. In 1814, an expedition from Halifax occupied the American territory of Maine.

THE TREATY OF GHENT

THIS IMAGE of the British and American envoys at Ghent commemorates the treaty that brought the British-American war to an end. By 1814, it had become clear that the war was going badly for both the British and the Americans. The British had not wanted to fight the war in the first place; the Americans were not winning it. Both sides wanted to end the war, but neither was prepared to accept a humiliating peace.

The Americans and British agreed to discuss peace in January 1814 but did not meet in Ghent, Belgium, until August, and then took until December to reach agreement. Captured territory would be returned, and a joint commission would settle boundary questions. The British had already ended their attempts to regulate American trade before the outbreak of war. They refused to renounce impressment, but the end of the European war with Napoleon in 1814 made this a moot point.

Most important, the British agreed to cut their ties to Native Americans. Native Americans were to regain the rights they had enjoyed before the war, but neither the British nor the Americans made a commitment to respect these rights in the future.

British and American representatives signed the Treaty of Ghent on Christmas Eve 1814. The Prince Regent ratified the treaty for the British on December 27, 1814; the American Senate ratified the treaty on February 17, 1815. The war officially ended that night at 11:00 PM.

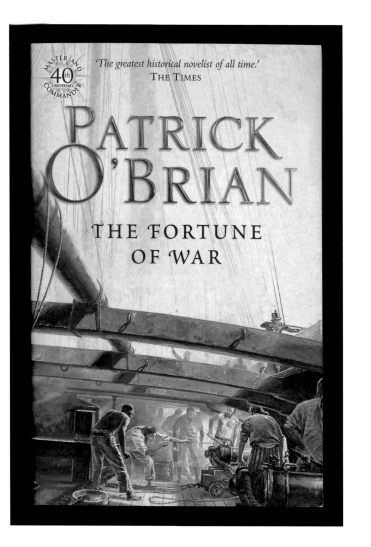

PATRICK O'BRIAN

THE FORTUNE OF WAR

FORGETTING THE WAR

When the British look back on the period of 1812 to 1815, the vast majority see the last years of a heroic era of struggle against the menace of revolutionary and Napoleonic France. During this era, great battles like Waterloo and Trafalgar shook the earth and sea; heroes like Horatio Nelson and the Duke of Wellington strode quarterdecks and battlefields like giants, fighting to defend the British Isles. Compared with the Napoleonic epic, a small war for small colonies across the Atlantic barely registered. The battles of the War of 1812, along with the war itself, are so completely forgotten by the British that they might never have happened at all.

For British consumers of popular culture, the War of 1812 now exists only in the pages of naval novels. Author Patrick O'Brian, in particular, sent his heroes, Jack Aubrey and Stephen Maturin, off to fight the Americans in a series of engagements that included HMS *Shannon*'s capture of the USS *Chesapeake*. Novelist C.S. Forrester, on the other hand, preferred to avoid the war altogether by sending Horatio Hornblower, the most famous fictional British naval officer in history, off to Russia to fight Napoleon. "If Hornblower were not safely employed up the Baltic," he wrote, "there was the danger (which I did not like to contemplate) that it would be his bombs that burst in the air over Baltimore."

3

THE CANADIAN WAR

The Americans were in high spirits and when I said
I was Canadian, one of the officers laughed and said "You'll soon
be under the Yankey government, my boy." I was sassy, like
most boys of my age, and I said, "I'm not so sure about that."

JACOB CLINE, thirteen years old, 1813

CANADA UNDER ATTACK

THIS HEAVILY romanticized painting of the Battle of Queenston Heights captures the essence of Canada's War of 1812. An American army had invaded Canada and taken post on Queenston Heights. Commanded by Major-General Sir Isaac Brock, forces of British regulars, French- and English-speaking militia, and First Peoples warriors stood together to defend Canada and triumph against the odds.

For modern Canadians, the War of 1812 is the epic story of the successful defence of a small colony under attack by a much larger neighbour. American invasions caused widespread suffering but never seriously threatened British control of Canada.

MAJOR-GENERAL SIR ISAAC BROCK
Isaac Brock led the defence of Upper Canada
during the first months of the War of 1812.

ISAAC BROCK

MAJOR-GENERAL SIR Isaac Brock was wearing this tunic when he was killed in action while leading a charge at the Battle of Queenston Heights. The hole left by the fatal musket ball is visible just below Brock's lapel.

FORCED TO FIGHT

Although painted in 1838, *Bush Farm near Chatham* features a backwoods farmstead that could just as easily have been situated in western New York state as Upper Canada in 1812.

When Britain and the United States went to war, Canada's proximity to the United States made it the principal theatre of a war in which Canadians had no real interest. Canadians had no grievances against the United States that were worth risking war. Upper Canada welcomed American immigrants, and many families had relatives on both sides of the border. Settler societies in Upper Canada and western New York were very similar and linked by close social and economic ties. War with America would threaten these connections and expose emerging communities to invasion and destruction.

Some Canadians thought that these connections should not be threatened by a British-American war. As a letter in the *Kingston Gazette* declared to the United States in 1812, "If your quarrel is with Britain, go and revenge yourselves upon her shores."

That notwithstanding, Canada was the only part of the British Empire that the United States could attack. Lack of a fleet strong enough to challenge the Royal Navy on the high seas, and the sheer distances involved, prevented the United States from either attacking Britain directly or launching amphibious assaults on the Atlantic colonies or Quebec City. Canada, on the other hand, lay just across the border.

AMERICAN INVASIONS

An AMERICAN soldier wore this coat during the War of 1812. The regular infantry that formed the core of most American armies wore blue or grey, just as British soldiers wore scarlet or green. For combatants of both sides, colourful uniforms reduced the chance of mistaking friends for enemies on battlefields wreathed in black powder smoke.

Americans in uniforms similar to this one launched eight major invasions of Canada during two and a half years of war. Neither the British nor the Americans won a decisive victory along the American-Canadian border. The Americans could not conquer Canada; the British could not destroy the American capacity for making war. But given the objectives of either side, as long as the British were not losing, they were winning, and as long as the Americans were not winning, they were losing.

DEFENDING CANADA

THE BATTLE of the Châteauguay remains one of the iconic engagements of Canada's War of 1812. In a conflict where most of the action occurred in Upper Canada (now Ontario), a key battle that took place south of Montreal has served for generations as a reminder that Lower Canada (now Quebec) came under American attack as well.

Charles Pinguet de Vaucour, a Châteauguay veteran, described his experience of the battle in a letter to his brother two weeks later.

Our soldiers fired between 35 and 40 cartridges, aimed so well that the prisoners we took the next day told us that our balls struck at the same height—between the head and the chest. Our company fought alone for about three quarters of an hour before we were reinforced. After the battle, we were sent back to our entrenchments where we passed a week of rain and cold without fire or shelter. We suffered so much, that several men fell sick every day. I now think that a man can endure more misery than a good dog.

During the War of 1812, a combination of British, colonial, and First Peoples forces won battles such as Châteauguay that saved Canada from American occupation. The Royal Navy guarded Canada's lines of communication. The British army provided tough, disciplined regulars who could stand in the line of battle. Many Canadians, Maritimers, and Newfoundlanders joined colonial regular regiments that fought alongside British regulars. Others served in the militia, transporting supplies, building fortifications, guarding prisoners, and occasionally engaging in combat. First Peoples warriors were superb skirmishers, sharpshooters, and scouts, whose mere presence frequently intimidated American troops.

CHARLES-MICHEL D'IRUMBERRY DE SALABERRY
Charles-Michel d'Irumberry de Salaberry led the Canadian
regulars and militia and First Peoples warriors who defeated an
American invasion at the Battle of the Châteauguay.

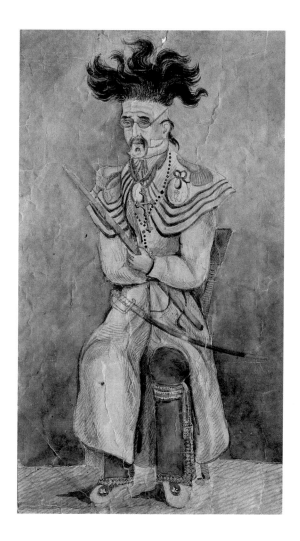

MOOKOMAANISH (LITTLE KNIFE)

Odawa war chief Mookomaanish (Little Knife) received a
presentation sword from the British after the War of 1812
in recognition of his humanity towards an American prisoner.

FIRST PEOPLES AT WAR

PADDLED BY figures representing distinguished chiefs and warriors who served in the War of 1812, this remarkable work of art was produced around 1820 by Odawa chief Jean-Baptiste Assiginack, himself a veteran of that conflict.

Among the paddlers were Mookomaanish and Blackbird. Assiginack described Mookomaanish as "an eminent war chief who distinguished himself in the late American war... with nine of his young men he fell upon a party of Americans, killed nine, took one prisoner, and received a severe wound in his knee," and Blackbird as "a very distinguished orator; he complains bitterly of the state of slavery to which his tribe are reduced since the war, their lands having been given up to the Americans."

Serving as independent allies of the British Crown, Canadian First Peoples from Lake Superior to the St. Lawrence valley chose when and how they would take part in the defence of Canada. As a result of these decisions, warriors played prominent and often decisive roles in some of the most celebrated engagements of the war, including Queenston Heights, Châteauguay, and Beaver Dams.

DEVASTATED LANDSCAPES

PERHAPS THE strangest artifact of the War of 1812 is this otherwise unremarkable book, *Sermons on Several Subjects by the Right Reverend Beilby Porteus*. Anglican minister Robert Addison of St. Mark's Church in Newark (Niagara-on-the-Lake, Ontario) borrowed the book from the local public library in 1812. American soldiers burned the town in 1813 and imprisoned Addison before he could return it. The book became part of the collection of the Addison Library attached to the church. Not until 2005 did the library staff realize that *Sermons on Several Subjects* was 193 years overdue.

Amusing as a library book almost two centuries overdue might sound, *Sermons on Several Subjects* is an artifact of the terrible suffering and loss many Canadians endured during the war.

The greater part of the fighting occurred along the Niagara and Detroit frontiers, in Upper Canada's four western counties. Here, American forces burned entire communities, including Newark, and looted and robbed at will. British troops stole food and tore down fences for firewood. Elsewhere in Lower and Upper Canada, the war remained a distant threat—most of the time.

The people of the Niagara frontier suffered most. Before the war, this was the most prosperous region in Upper Canada. "Most of the original log houses had given place to good frame buildings," wrote resident Amelia Harris, "and the inhabitants generally seemed prosperous and content when the war broke out."

Lower Canadian Thomas-René-Verchères Boucher de Boucherville, who served as a volunteer in Upper Canada during the war, had an entirely different

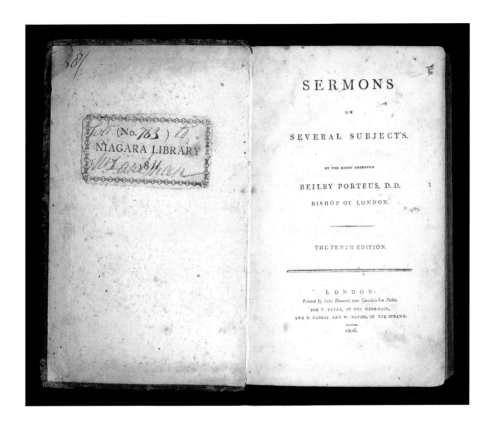

SERMONS

ON

SEVERAL SUBJECTS.

BY THE RIGHT REVEREND

BEILBY PORTEUS, D.D.

BISHOP OF LONDON.

THE TENTH EDITION.

LONDON:
Printed by Luke Hansard, near Lincoln's-Inn Fields,
FOR T. PAYNE, AT THE MEWS-GATE,
AND T. CADELL AND W. DAVIES, IN THE STRAND.
1806.

perspective when he passed through Niagara in 1815. "Everywhere I saw devastation," he wrote, "homes in ashes, fields trampled and laid waste, forts demolished, forests burned and blackened, truly a most pitiful sight." An American visitor two years later had the same impression: "Where peace and plenty once abounded, poverty and destruction now stalked the land."

ATLANTIC CANADA'S WAR

THIS VERY rare image of a Canadian privateer from the War of 1812 shows HMS *Martin* capturing the American privateer the *Snap Dragon*. Privateers were privately owned warships that attempted to capture enemy ships and sell the vessels and their cargos. In this case, entrepreneurs from Saint John, New Brunswick, bought the American vessel and sent it back out to sea as the *Snapdragon* to prey on American commerce.

For Maritimers and Newfoundlanders, participation in the War of 1812 meant sending privateers to sea and colonial regulars to Canada. Nova Scotia and New Brunswick residents, supported by their governors, remained neutral and maintained normal commercial relations with New England for as long as possible. This did not prevent many individuals from the Atlantic region from enlisting in colonial regular regiments that served in local garrisons or in Canada.

VICTORY THROUGH SURVIVAL

BRITISH REGULARS armed with India Pattern muskets like this one played a key role in defending Canada during the War of 1812, a war that Canada won not by defeating the United States, but simply by remaining part of the British Empire.

That hostilities ended with Canada still in British hands represented a victory for Anglophones, Francophones, and First Peoples who wanted nothing more than to get on with their lives. The successful defence of Canada allowed British North America to evolve into a free and independent transcontinental country.

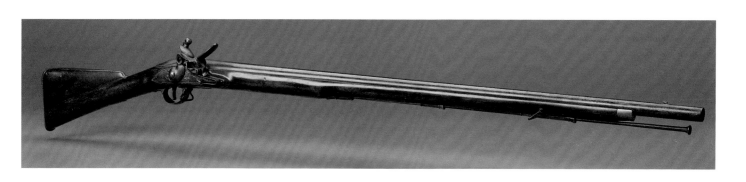

4

THE NATIVE AMERICAN WAR

Here is a chance presented to us; yes, such as will never occur again, for us Indians of North America to form ourselves into one great combination, and cast our lot with the British in this war.

TECUMSEH, 1812

A CLASH OF CIVILIZATIONS

IF THERE is one hero of the War of 1812 who is admired and respected by all sides, it is Tecumseh, portrayed on this Shawnee coin. His reputation among contemporary Canadians is revealed in a letter from a Canadian settler to his brother in June of 1813. As an American army advanced towards Hamilton, he wrote, "I wish we had Tecumseh here to help us out of our difficulties."

For the Americans and British, the War of 1812 was a conflict between governments that began in 1812 and ended in 1815. For Tecumseh and Native Americans from the Great Lakes to the Gulf of Mexico, it was a clash of civilizations. Their War of 1812 was just one element of a long struggle by Native Americans to adjust to life on a continent that was increasingly dominated by European settlers and the colonies and countries that they had founded.

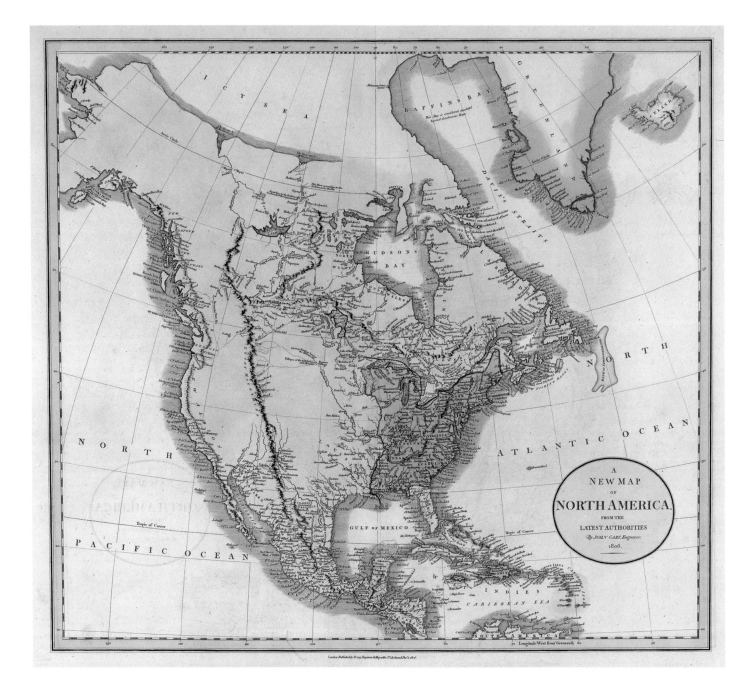

A
NEW MAP
OF
NORTH AMERICA,
FROM THE
LATEST AUTHORITIES
By JOHN CARY, Engraver.
1806.

UNDER ATTACK

THIS 1806 map showing the boundaries of the United States overflowing into Native American territory provides a dramatic illustration of the ongoing threat facing these nations. First British and then American settlers had been expanding into Native American homelands for centuries. Ever since the first British settlements appeared on the eastern seaboard in the early 1600s, settlers had been building a continental empire. Always driving west (and occasionally north), they overwhelmed or displaced the Native American nations in their path and converted Native American homelands into British colonies or American states.

Native Americans responded by forming coalitions that generally combined spiritual and cultural renewal with military resistance. Faced with both cultural challenges and physical invasions, Native Americans between the Appalachian Mountains and the Mississippi River began to think on a continental scale. New religious movements portrayed Native Americans as a single people with common interests who could gain power by following revitalized pre-contact lifestyles. New alliances brought nations together to hold off American settlers.

TECHNOLOGY AND ALLIANCE

MUSKETS LIKE this one, made in Britain for presentation to distinguished allied leaders, increased the military power of Native American nations but also made them dependent upon European technology.

Europeans had not just invaded and colonized vast chunks of North America, they had also globalized Native American warfare. Pre-contact native nations could make war using their own resources. The introduction of European firearms made that impossible. To fight a war, Native Americans needed not just imported weapons but also reliable supplies of powder and shot and access to technicians who could repair muskets. To fight a European power, they needed allies who could fill gaps in their military capability by contributing cannon to batter down fortifications and regular troops who could face European-style armies in the field.

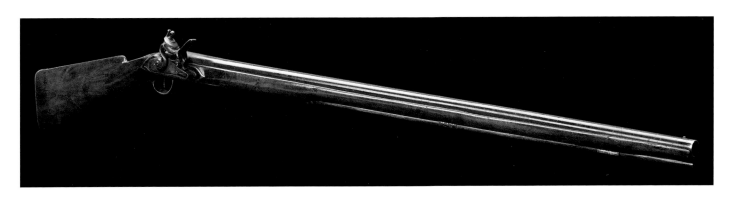

THE GREAT COALITION

The formation of the last great Native American coalition of the period began in 1805 when Shawnee mystic Tenskwatawa (facing), Tecumseh's brother, led a new religious revival that quickly evolved into a powerful military alliance. When it came to the United States, Tenskwatawa's followers did not mince words. Speaking at Mackinac in 1805, Ojibwa envoy Le Maigouis passed on Tenskwatawa's spiritual and political message.

> The Great Spirit bids me to address you in his own words, which are these:...
> I am the father of the English, of the French, of the Spanish, and of the Indi-
> ans... But the Americans I did not make. They are not my children but the
> children of the Evil Spirit ... They are numerous and I hate them. They are
> unjust. They have taken away your lands, which were not made for them.

Americans responded to this coalition and attempts by Tenskwatawa and Tecumseh to prevent sales of Native American land to the United States by striking first. On November 7, 1811, an American army led by William Henry Harrison, governor of Indiana, defeated a coalition force at the Battle of Tippecanoe. Although shaken by this defeat, the coalition remained intact.

Nonetheless, the Native American strategic situation was becoming critical. Every attempt to halt American westward expansion had failed. And Britain, the only European power within reach, vastly preferred peace with the United States to alliance with Native Americans.

Then the United States declared war on Great Britain and everything changed.

THE BRITISH ALLIANCE

Medals like this, bearing an image of King George III and presented by the British to Native American leaders, symbolized friendship, alliance, and a chance to secure their national territories.

For Native Americans, Great Britain's danger was their opportunity. Huron oral tradition records Tecumseh's response to the outbreak of war. Tecumseh, who evidently assumed that the British intended to bring the United States back under their control, declared:

> Here is a chance presented to us; yes, such as will never occur again, for us Indians of North America to form ourselves into one great combination, and cast our lot with the British in this war; and should they conquer and again get the mastery of the whole of North America, our rights... would be respected by the King.

To align themselves with the British was to take a desperate chance. Their new ally had failed to overcome American rebels during the War of Independence, lacked the power to protect their interests during the peace negotiations, and failed to support their former comrades-in-arms in subsequent wars with the United States.

But it was their only chance. Joining the British-American war offered at least the hope that alliance with Britain would allow Native Americans to win their own war against the United States.

THE WAR IN THE NORTH

THE NATIVE AMERICAN war had begun well but ended in defeat beside the Thames River in western Upper Canada on October 5, 1813. This stylized, pro-American representation of the Battle of the Thames (or Moraviantown) portrays American cavalry riding down British regulars and Native American warriors. When the British regulars broke and fled, Native Americans led by Tecumseh stood their ground until he was killed and the weight of numbers forced the warriors to retreat.

For Native Americans, the War of 1812 had commenced with Tecumseh leading an army north to participate in the defence of Upper Canada. This army played a key role in defending Canada during the first phase of the war. In 1812, the capture by Native Americans of a supply train helped to compel the Americans to abandon their first attempt to conquer Canada. A few weeks later, they took part in the British capture of Detroit. By the end of the campaign, about one thousand warriors had joined Tecumseh. Farther west, other British and Native American forces seized key posts in the northwest and occupied what is now Wisconsin. Native American attempts to secure their own territory were less successful, and attempts to capture other American forts in 1813 failed dismally.

The American naval victory on Lake Erie forced the British to evacuate southwestern Upper Canada. The subsequent Battle of the Thames and the inability of the British to decisively defeat the Americans ended the Native Americans' hopes of parlaying an alliance with Britain into security for their homelands.

A Drawing of the Muscogie Chief Francis of himself; being his first attempt; and never having seen a pencil or so too in his life before.

THE WAR IN THE SOUTH

In 1811, Muscogee (Creek) spiritual leader Hillis Hadjo (Josiah Francis) met and became a supporter of Tecumseh. Two years later, Hadjo became one of the leaders of a second Native American War of 1812. Fear of continuing American encroachments, the construction of a road through their territory, and the emergence of a pro-American faction within the Muscogee Nation led the warriors known as Red Sticks to strike back at the United States.

Their capture of Fort Mims, Alabama, shocked Americans, but future president Andrew Jackson defeated the Red Sticks at the Battle of Horseshoe Bend in Alabama in 1814. The British did not make contact with the Red Sticks until after that battle and failed to provide any effective support.

facing:
HILLIS HADJO (JOSIAH FRANCIS)
Hillis Hadjo (Josiah Francis), a leader of the Muscogee (Creek)
Red Stick movement that fought against the United States during the War
of 1812, painted this self-portrait while on a diplomatic mission to Britain.

THE ONGOING STRUGGLE

THIS SHAWNEE NATION silver dollar commemorates the Trail of Tears, the expulsion of many Native American groups from their homelands east of the Mississippi River following the passage in Washington of the Indian Removal Act in 1830.

For Native Americans, the War of 1812 was a catastrophe that shattered both the Tenskwatawa and Tecumseh coalitions and the Red Stick movement and led to the withdrawal of British support for their struggle for freedom and independence. Native Americans were never again able to find external allies or threaten to roll back the American frontier.

This did not prevent them from continuing to work to preserve their heritage.

SHINGWAUKONSE

SHINGWAUKONSE, SEATED in the middle in this photograph, was a veteran of Tecumseh's coalition and chief of the Ojibwa of Garden River, located in Upper Canada near Sault Ste. Marie. He and other Native American leaders used diplomacy to attempt to secure economic and political independence for their communities.

THE WHITECAP DAKOTA

Service as British allies in the War of 1812 remains an important part of the history of the Whitecap Dakota First Nation, which produced this calendar to commemorate its role in the war. When the Whitecap First Nation came to Canada in 1862, following an unsuccessful war with the United States, Chief Wapahaska showed Canadian officials an alliance medal (similar to the one on p. 80) dating back to the War of 1812 to remind them of his nation's longstanding relationship with the Crown.

EPILOGUE

In 1914, an American arts society issued this medallion to commemorate the anniversary of the negotiation of the Treaty of Ghent. The Latin inscriptions on the front and back mean "The last war between brothers" and "Peace for one hundred years."

The War of 1812 proved to be the last armed conflict between Great Britain and the United States. When the war ended, British-American relations went back to normal, with intervals of tension occurring against a background of trade, investment, and immigration. Both sides fortified the Canadian-American border and their respective Atlantic coasts, but they agreed to limit warship construction on the Great Lakes and Lake Champlain. The British built the Rideau Canal to serve as a secure wartime transportation link between Montreal and Upper Canada. The Treaty of Washington of 1871 resolved issues that had nearly caused a British-American war during the American Civil War and ushered in a period of growing cooperation and, later, alliance between Canada, the United States, and Great Britain that has lasted up to the present.

Wars between the United States and Native Americans, who were unable after 1815 to seek the support of a powerful foreign ally, continued until the late nineteenth century.

A war pitting Canada, Great Britain, and Native Americans against the United States is now unthinkable. But this does not stop the descendants of two of the four participants in the war, Canadians and Americans, from continuing to agree to disagree about who won the War of 1812.

For Canadians, their victory is self-evident. The combined force of British, Canadians, and First Peoples may have lost the occasional battle, but the fact that maple leaf flags fly across the continent and north to Ellesmere Island proclaims that Canada won the war.

For Americans, it is a little more complicated. They never broke the British blockade and never came close to conquering Canada. But they did succeed, for the most part, in defending American territory against British attacks. For Americans, that has been more than enough for them to regard this conflict as an American triumph.

Preserving their own versions of events gives both Americans and Canadians a satisfying view of the War of 1812. Comparing perspectives provides a more comprehensive understanding of their shared history.

FURTHER READING

Benn, Carl, *The War of 1812*. Oxford: Osprey, 2002.

Ibid., *The Iroquois in the War of 1812*. Toronto: University of Toronto Press, 1998.

Chartrand, René, *British Forces in North America, 1793–1815*. Oxford: Osprey, 1998.

Graves, Dianne, *In the Midst of Alarms: The Untold Story of Women and the War of 1812*. Toronto: Robin Brass Studio, 2007.

Guitard, Michelle, *Histoire sociale des miliciens de la bataille de la Châteauguay*. Ottawa: Parks Canada, 1983.

Hickey, Donald R., *Don't Give Up the Ship!: Myths of the War of 1812*. Champaign, IL: University of Illinois Press, 2006.

Hitsman, J. Mackay, updated by Donald E. Graves, *The Incredible War of 1812: A Military History*. Toronto: Robin Brass Studio, 1999, revised edition.

Klinck, Carl F., and James J. Talman, eds., *The Journal of Major John Norton, 1816*. Toronto: The Champlain Society, 1970.

Latimer, Jon, *1812: War with America*. Cambridge, MA: The Belknap Press of Harvard University Press, 2007.

Mantle, Craig Leslie, ed., *Les apathiques et les rebelles: Des exemples canadiens de mutinerie et de désobéissance*. Toronto: Dundurn, 2007, translation of *The Unwilling and the Reluctant: Theoretical Perspectives on Disobedience in the Military*. Winnipeg: Canadian Defence Academy Press, 2006.

Stanley, George F.G., *La guerre de 1812: Les opérations terrestres*. Montreal: Éditions du Trécarré and National Museum of Man, 1984, translation of *The War of 1812: Land Operations*. Toronto: Macmillan of Canada and the National Museum of Man, 1983.

Taylor, Alan, *The Civil War of 1812: American Citizens, British Subjects, Irish Rebels, and Indian Allies*. New York: Knopf, 2010.

IMAGE CREDITS

D. PETER MACLEOD is the pre-Confederation historian at the Canadian War Museum, where he curated the exhibition *1812*. A longstanding student of eighteenth-century Canada, he is the author of *The Canadian Iroquois and the Seven Years' War* (published in French as *Les Iroquois et la guerre de sept ans*) and *Northern Armageddon: The Battle of the Plains of Abraham* (published in French as *La vérité sur la bataille des Plaines d'Abraham*). He lives in Ottawa, Ontario.